MW01000007

Lulu the Lamb loved to laugh.

Lulu laughed at Ladybug
because she was so little.

Lulu laughed at Llama when he spilled pink lemonade at lunch.

Lulu laughed at Lizard
when she fell off the ladder.

Lulu laughed at Leopard's lavender leotard.

The other animals did not like Lulu's laughing.
It made them feel low.
"Someday, Lulu will learn," said Leopard.

Lulu walked along, laughing loudly.
She bumped into Lion, who was licking a lollipop.
The lollipop got stuck in Lion's mane!

Lulu laughed at Lion.
She laughed and laughed and laughed.

Lion looked angry. He roared at Lulu.
Lion roared so loud, he made Lulu fall...
right into the lake!

Ladybug, Llama, Lizard, Leopard, and Lion laughed at Lulu.
Lulu didn't like being laughed at one little bit!

"From now on, I will laugh less,"
Lulu promised her friends.
"At last, Lulu has learned her lesson!"
said Ladybug.

Lulu still likes to laugh at her friends...

but only when they tell her a funny joke!

14

See inside back cover for answers.

Ll Cheer

L is for lamb and licorice stick

L is for lots of lollipops to lick

L is for lion and ladybug

L is for leaf and lemonade in a jug

Hooray for L, big and small—

the loveliest, luckiest letter of all!